How Things Work:
Remote Control Planes

by Joanne M

Content Cons

Nanci R. Vargus, Ed.D.
Professor Emeritus, University of Indianapolis

Reading Consultant

Jeanne M. Clidas, Ph.D.
Reading Specialist

Children's Press®
An Imprint of Scholastic Inc.

Library of Congress Cataloging-in-Publication Data
Mattern, Joanne, 1963- author.
  Remote controlled planes / by Joanne Mattern.
    pages cm. -- (Rookie read-about science. How things work)
  Summary: "Introduces the reader to remote control planes."-- Provided by publisher.
  ISBN 978-0-531-21369-8 (library binding) -- ISBN 978-0-531-21457-2 (pbk.) 1. Remote control--Juvenile
literature. 2. Airplanes--Models--Radio control--Juvenile literature. 3. Drone aircraft--Juvenile literature.
4. Vehicles, Remotely piloted--Juvenile literature. I. Title.

  TL770.M374 2016
  629.132'6--dc23   2015018070

Produced by Spooky Cheetah Press
Design by Keith Plechaty

© 2016 by Scholastic Inc.

All rights reserved. Published in 2016 by Children's Press, an imprint of Scholastic Inc.

Printed in China 62

SCHOLASTIC, CHILDREN'S PRESS, ROOKIE READ-ABOUT®, and associated logos are trademarks and/or
registered trademarks of Scholastic Inc.

1 2 3 4 5 6 7 8 9 10 R 25 24 23 22 21 20 19 18 17 16

Photographs ©: cover: Wayne Forward/Media Bakery; 3 top left: Margo Harrison/Shutterstock, Inc.;
3 top right: Tatiana Popova/Shutterstock, Inc.; 3 bottom: Cosmin Sava/Shutterstock, Inc.; 4: Ghislain &
Marie David de Lossy; 7: View Stock/Getty Images; 8: Kuttig - People/Alamy Images; 11: Robert McGouey/
Alamy Images; 15: Gunter Nezhoda/Alamy Images; 16: Archive Holdings Inc./Getty Images; 19: Jay Smith/
Model Aviation magazine; 20: Natasha Quarmby/Demotix/Corbis Images; 23: MiriamPolito/Thinkstock;
24: Amazon/UPI/Newscom; 26-27 background: vladimir salman/Shutterstock, Inc.; 26 top: Vudhikrai/
Shutterstock, Inc.; 26 center left, 26 center right: Tatiana Popova/Shutterstock, Inc.; 26 bottom: Kenneth
Graff/Shutterstock, Inc.; 27 top left: Slava Shishkin/Shutterstock, Inc.; 27 top right: Stocktrek Images/
Thinkstock; 27 center left, 27 center right: surawutob/Shutterstock, Inc.; 30 top, 30 bottom: Mike Blake/
Reuters/Landov; 31 top: MiriamPolito/Thinkstock; 31 center top: Robert McGouey/Alamy Images; 31 center
bottom: Kuttig - People/Alamy Images; 31 bottom: Tatiana Popova/Shutterstock, Inc.

Illustrations by Jeffrey Chandler/Art Gecko Studios!

Table of Contents

Soaring Through the Sky

Buzzz… Zzzoom! Remote control planes zip across the sky. They can fly high and fast. But there is not a tiny person inside the plane making it zoom ahead. How can a remote control airplane actually fly?

The Pilot in Charge

In real airplanes, the **pilot** sits in front. He or she controls how the plane flies. But in a remote control plane, the pilot is on the ground.

The pilot controls the **transmitter**. The transmitter sends radio signals to the plane. These signals tell the plane where to fly.

FUN FACT!

Each part of the plane has its own control on the transmitter.

The signals go to a part inside the plane called a receiver.

The pilot wants the plane to fly higher or lower. She presses a few buttons on the transmitter. The signals go to the receiver. The plane goes up or down.

Parts of a Plane

A remote control plane has a lot of the same parts as a real plane. First, it has wings and an engine.

The engine makes the plane move through the air. As the plane flies, something called **lift** pushes up on the wings. Lift helps keep the plane in the air.

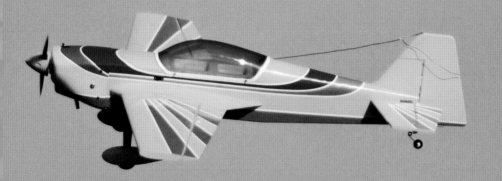

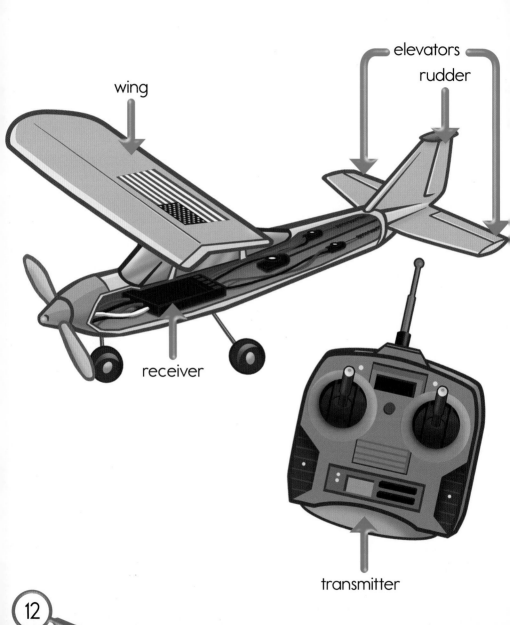

elevators

rudder

wing

receiver

transmitter

12

The back of the plane has two parts called elevators. They make the plane go up or down. The elevators are controlled by the pilot using the transmitter.

Another part is called the rudder.
It is also in the back of the plane.
The pilot uses the transmitter to
send a "turn" signal to the plane.
The rudder moves left or right
to turn the plane in the proper
direction.

rudder

EXTRA 260

1940s

The First Remote Control Planes

When people started to build airplanes, inventors made small model planes. They used them to test whether the real planes would work. Soon children were playing with these model planes.

Later, inventors added engines to the models. But how could they control the planes?

Two brothers named Walter and William Good had an idea. They thought that the best way to fly the little planes would be to use a remote control.

The brothers built the first successful remote control plane in 1937. They named it "Big Guff." Big Guff made more than 1,000 flights!

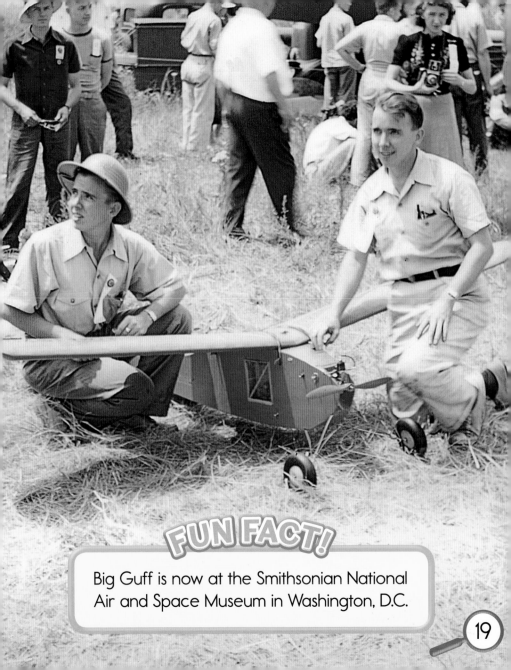

FUN FACT!

Big Guff is now at the Smithsonian National Air and Space Museum in Washington, D.C.

So Many Planes!

Today there are many kinds of remote control planes. Some are just for fun. They come in all different sizes—from very small to really big. Some remote control pilots get together to fly their planes at festivals.

Some remote control planes are called **drones**. A drone is sent into the air by a transmitter. Then the pilot uses a computer to control it.

Some people attach cameras to their planes. The planes take pictures of the ground below.

People can use drones to test the weather. They can warn people when storms, such as hurricanes, are heading their way.

camera

quad copter

Some companies use remote control planes to deliver packages. These drones may be able to deliver packages faster than trucks can.

There is no telling where you might see a remote control plane flying in the future!

FUN FACT!

A quad copter is a remote control helicopter with four rotors.
The word *quad* means "four."

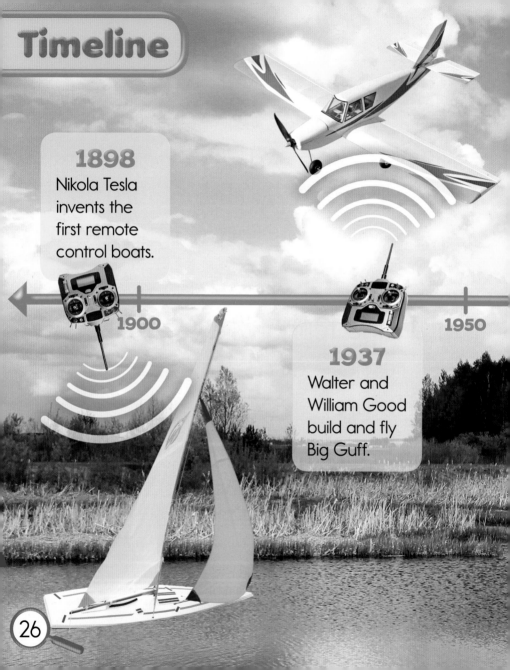

Timeline

1898
Nikola Tesla invents the first remote control boats.

1900

1937
Walter and William Good build and fly Big Guff.

1950

1968
Dieter Schlüterumlaut builds the first remote control helicopter.

2000

2012
One out of every three planes in the U.S. Air Force is an unmanned remote control plane.

Super Science

Ask an adult for help. Do not attempt this science experiment on your own!

Air flows over and under an airplane's wings. Because of the shape of the wing, the lighter air goes over the wing. The heavier air goes underneath. That provides lift. This experiment will show how air and a plane's wings work together to create lift.

You Will Need: One sheet of 8½" x 11" paper

1.
Fold the paper in half along the longer side. Make sure the fold is nice and sharp!

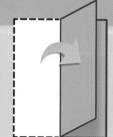

2.
Unfold the paper. Fold the two top corners toward the middle fold. The two outer edges of the paper should touch each other at the fold line.

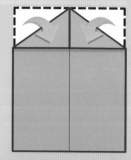

3.

Fold the paper in half along the vertical fold you made in step #1.

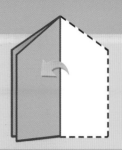

4.

Fold the wings down, one side at a time. Try to launch your plane into the air.

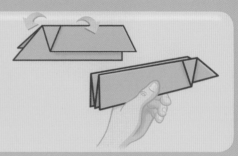

5.

Now unfold the wings so they stick out from the body of the plane. Try to fly your plane again.

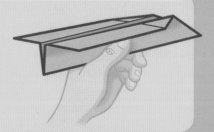

Why This Works:

When the plane's wings are not extended, heavier air cannot flow underneath them. There is nothing there for the air to "lift" up against.

That's Amazing!

Look. Up in the sky. Is it a bird? Is it a plane?

Actually it is Flyguy. That is the name given to the radio controlled superhero created by Otto Dieffenbach.

Dieffenbach used to be a test pilot for the U.S. Air Force. He started flying remote control planes when he was a little boy. Several years ago, Dieffenbach designed his Flyguys, which include Superman and Iron Man.

Flyguys are made of foam and they have a propeller, just like a remote control airplane. The superheroes' flat feet act like rudders, so they are easy to steer. Doesn't that sound super?

Glossary

drones (DROHNZ): aircraft that fly without pilots on board

lift (LIFT): force that makes a plane rise into the air

pilot (PYE-luht): someone who flies an aircraft

transmitter (tranz-MIT-uhr): something that sends a signal to a receiver

Index

Facts for Now

Visit this Scholastic Web site for more information on remote control planes:
www.factsfornow.scholastic.com
Enter the keywords **Remote Control Planes**

About the Author

Joanne Mattern is the author of many nonfiction books for children. Science is one of her favorite subjects to write about! She lives in New York State with her husband, four children, and numerous pets.